CW01671691

LOVE IS ALL THERE IS

A PERSONAL GUIDE TO MAGNIFICENCE

RYAN LEE CHOW

© 2012 RYAN LEE CHOW

All rights reserved. This book may not be reproduced in whole or in part, or transmitted in any form, or by any means electronic, mechanical, photocopying, recording, or other, without written permission from the author Ryan Lee Chow.

LOVE
IS ALL
THERE IS

TO THE LOVE AND LIGHT WE ALL ARE

FOREWORD

Love is encoded in every chapter of our lives

I have been looking for answers for many years, praying, believing that there will be someone to help me; to save me. I asked myself infinite times; what is love? Where, when and how can I feel the love without compromising who I am?

I couldn't find the answers. I was expecting love to be in a specific form without seeing the magnificence that was hidden in every person and event that surrounded me.

Ryan's guide to magnificence 'Love is all there is' is a delicacy, a masterpiece and a reencounter with that essence we all have; an awakening to our inner truth.

I have read many books, amazing 'best sellers' and 'self help bibles' and none of them has showed me with such a clarity how to take new steps in my life and how to follow my heart. This is an amazing book that will surely show you your way back home.

The journey in this book is narrated in a unique way and expressed with gracefulness and harmony while intelligence is embedded throughout these pages. You are guided to look inside of yourself, where you will find and see your true magnificence in a very direct and simple way.

Ryan's gift is helping others to see their 'true essence' and this goes beyond self help books or the mastering of disciplines. This is something that is genuinely inside each one of us and once you see it you will never look back.

His life is most inspiring and he is a true example that has walked his talk from the very beginning. He has always been on the path of helping others to see that inner perfection, with a commitment and discipline that clearly shows what his mission is; enlighten the world.

We all have a message encoded in our hearts: love, connect and share. Nothing can give you more satisfaction! That is the message you will rediscovered at the end of this book.

Our society is run by the illusion that one day happiness will be found and there will be no more so called 'problems'. We look every day and can't seem to find it; it becomes elusive. Then, after a few encounters with challenges we stop pursuing our goals and start living afraid of life, living subordinated to fears and to the quick pleasures that society offers instead.

Ryan's teachings throughout these pages are an authentic, pure and essential truth that will guide you to a life where you will see, feel and express that love is all there is and it does not matter where you are now or what others tell you because you already follow what your heart says.

We all have an inner gift to be expressed, something that if we wouldn't express it the world will be missing something and it is in that very living when the world conspires with all its capacities to wake us up to that inner gift, that is what we live for, that is what we call challenges, that is what we fear at times and is nothing but the expression of love.

I am absolutely delighted and grateful to have the privilege to write a foreword for an incredible person and friend whose teachings rise beyond paradigms and theories and communicate purely with ones soul, giving us direct access to the spark of light that shines within you.

Much Love,

Frank Arrigazzi,
Longevity Advisor and Yoga Teacher;
Founder of Purple Balance Superfoods
www.purplebalancesuperfoods.com

CONTENTS

INTRODUCTION

I'm going ask you a simple yet powerful question...

What is the one thing that can always make you smile? It could be a song, a line from a film, a piece of art, your partner, your child, your mum's hug, your pet, or even your plants... it could be anything that has the power to make you smile. Close your eyes and think about this one thing for a moment...

Excellent!

It is my sincere wish for you to have that same smile about your entire life by the time you finish reading this book.

Along my journey I've been deeply inspired by learning and being able to teach others about what I truly believe in.

My life is dedicated to understanding the mysteries behind, beyond and within life and my divine purpose here on earth is to shine a light on the path of fulfilment to help guide people to see and appreciate their own magnificence. To see through the fears and limitations that appear to be blocking us from living our dreams.

I would love to share this journey and these experiences with you so we may all live in a wonderful world full of love and peace.

Thank you for choosing me to help guide you on your path to inner balance, magnificence and love. I am truly blessed to have this opportunity to share these lessons with you and wish you all the best in life and beyond.

I love you with all my heart,

Ryan Lee Chow

FOLLOW YOUR INSPIRATION

A long time ago, a dear friend of mine told me that when we are born, we are given a book with blank pages and it is up to us to write the story within this book. I thought, 'What type of book do I want to write? What adventures would I like to read in there? Which love stories will echo throughout my pages? How do I want to be remembered? This sparked the desire to live my life according to my heart.' My question to you now is, 'what type of book do you want to write with your life?'

- A book of love?
- Success?
- Epic adventures?
- Travel?
- Service?
- Fame?
- Peace?

Think about this and always remember, only you can write your story: make it as compelling as you like, it is your book and only you hold the power to write within it.

PART1

The first part of this book is written with a short story 'The journey' interwoven with important life secrets and lessons.

Chapter 1

THE JOURNEY BEGINS... THE ILLUSION

Not long ago there was a man, called David, who was desperately seeking help to find happiness and love in his life. He was almost always frustrated and depressed about everything and found little or no joy in his daily existence.

He had no enthusiasm about his weekdays, which were filled with working at a job that he didn't like, for people he didn't care for; he sometimes looked forward to the weekends just to drink and forget it all. He didn't really see any purpose to living anymore if this was all life could be. He felt insignificant and taken for granted.

Life was so monotonous, so predictable, and so empty that he was looking for any way out.

David was an intelligent man but his wife seemed to be separated from his life and he was constantly ill, always taking medicine and visiting his doctor. He didn't like his job, which paid badly and was boring; most of his friends made fun of him; and he rarely saw his family.

He thought, 'What a horrible life'; he was constantly in the same cycle just waiting for the end of the month to get his salary, even though all his money seemed to go on paying the bills.

He thought, 'What could have possibly gone wrong with my life?' He had got married when he was supposed to, he was working in a job his family wanted him to and he was a law abiding citizen.

As he had a good pension fund set up, he thought maybe he should just be patient and wait until he was 65 to enjoy life.

Maybe that was the answer!

THE ILLUSION

With so many distractions, manmade laws, false beliefs, unhealthy foods and created authorities, it is very easy to fall into the illusion of physical reality rather than the truth of divinity and immortality.

The illusion is what we learnt and believed life to be. It is the source of fear and limitation which we adopt even without knowing we are subjecting ourselves to the disempowering system.

We are so much more!

As children we look to our parents and teachers for guidance and acceptance, learning whatever we can from them as they teach us and take care of us.

From the moment we begin to understand language and emotions, we develop the ego, personality and beliefs.

As these areas develop we start feeling the need to be significant and important to those around us. We begin listening to the opinions of others and make adjustments to our views and actions in order to feel accepted in these situations.

It is then that our thoughts and actions become influenced by these opinions and we begin living a life which is not true to our hearts.

We tend to do what we think we should in order to make our parents, teachers, friends proud even if it means doing something we don't like.

Because of these influences we tend to live in the shadows of others just to please them and not ourselves. As a result, we live a life which is not ours and not fulfilling.

We therefore live in suppression, regression, insignificance and false fears instead of inspiration, love and magnificence.

How many times do we remember hearing things like, you have to do this, you can't do that, that's wrong, don't be silly, etc?

At other times these words can be even harsher, accompanied by abusive actions which can easily add to more suppressed emotions resulting in greater emotional damage.

Of course, most of the time our parents and teachers only say these things because they love us and this is what they have learnt from their parents. They teach us the only way they know how to.

Remember they are human as well and have 'stuff' to deal with and are engrained with these ways because of their experiences and circumstances. Because we look up to them, we don't know any better either and at times can become disempowered. There is perfection and balance to this once one understands the divine order that exists!

There is no right or wrong, only lessons and gratitude! Our feelings do guide us to what is best for us and we always have choice and freewill.

When we surrender ourselves unknowingly to the created system, we give away all of our power before we even know there is a choice. The choice is to live in fear or live in love.

When we live in fear, we have a false outlook on the gift of life and we live in an illusion of limitation and pain.

When we are able to see through the false layers of restricting rules, manmade laws, created religions and limited beliefs that are imposed onto us, we have then begun to see the truth and beauty of life and can therefore reawaken to the power that exists within all of us. Let's now journey together to see how truly magnificent we are!

Let's be our own authorities!

Let's realise our unique divine purpose!

Let's become who we are really meant to be!

Chapter 2

THE JOURNEY CONTINUED… WILLING TO CHANGE

David knew something was missing as he looked around his room and realised that there was nothing else he could buy to make himself happy. He was so accustomed to spending all of his saved money on unnecessary things he would never really use.

One day while going home, he felt so distressed and depressed, he just wanted to spend some time talking with someone but realised there was no one to talk to, not even his wife was much in his life anymore. Everyone was gone and he had all these things with no one to share it with; his life was empty.

In an attempt to forget it all, he finished an open bottle of wine and then threw it across the room.

Finally, he dropped to his knees and tears poured down his face.

'Why? Why me? I work so hard and have nothing.

Life just isn't fair!'

He looked up and saw a picture of his dad on the wall. He loved his dad so much and had felt so alone the day he died, and even more so now.

At that same moment, he remembered a story his dad had told him as a child. He remembered very clearly his words.

'Son, there is a very wise old man who lives on the top of a mountain and knows the secret of life. My son, in this world, there may be a point in your life where you forget your true self and you may need to visit him to remember it. The only way you can visit him is if you are ready and willing to change; it is only then that you will know the path to fulfilment.'

David remembered himself as a boy, so happy and so free while hugging his dad. 'Tell me more tell me more,' he had said, 'where is the wise old man?' His father smiled peacefully and said, 'you will find him only if you are ready.'

David, now sitting on the ground holding the picture of his dad, said in a humble and genuine voice, 'I'm ready Dad, I'm willing to change'. He leaned back against his sofa and his thoughts drifted off.

WILLING TO CHANGE

This illusion of life happens to almost everyone at some point in time and we feel the pressure, stress and depression it can easily lead to.

It is at this time we can feel pain and lose our true sense of where we should be and sometimes look for an extreme way out.

Some people turn to alcohol, drugs or even worse to escape. We ask the question why? Why me? And feel empty inside. We feel a lack of passion for anything and just continue what feels like a monotonous life. Does this sound familiar?

Is this how you want to be?

Some of us feel these burdens and know there is something better but we live on without changing because of the illusion that this is how it was meant to be. We think this is how life really is!

Life becomes a struggle, ruled by dictators we are not consciously aware of and as a result we exist in inferiority, jumping into a sea of turmoil with no destination to swim to.

This is not life!

This is the illusion that is imposed unconsciously and sometimes purposefully onto us from an early age. An illusion strengthened by psychological interferences through brainwashing media, one-sided laws, power driven governments, etc.

Just think for a couple of minutes of other powerful influences we may have had growing up and they will start to become very visible. Schools? Religions? Films?

We can let go of these old beliefs of imposed fallacies and see the truth. Sometimes the truth is right before our eyes but because of these illusive layers, it is sometimes easy to become blinded and disempowered by the false information we have been taught.

As we only use on average 10 percent of our brains, what is the other 90 percent doing? We can awaken this area as we begin to understand the inner power we possess.

Let the beliefs that we aren't good enough drift away, let the beliefs that we are insignificant disappear, let the beliefs that we are nobodies dissolve. The question is, are you ready and willing to change?

Will you do what it takes?

I remember a story of a Qigong master who said, 'Come to this park every morning at 7:00 for 3 years, then I will teach you!'

It is not the actually waiting for 3 years that determines if we are ready or not, it is the state of mind for really wanting to learn; the willingness to wait for 3 years because you know there is something amazing at the end of it; this is what really matters. The willingness to do whatever it takes to change is what makes the difference.

Do you have the willingness to change no matter what? If you do then the future is yours!

Are you ready to leave the darkness and soar into the realms of multidimensional light? Are you ready to leave the state of inferiority and live in the truth of magnificence? Are you ready to leave the illusion of false reality and live in the splendour of pure divinity?

If the answer is a YES then get ready for a magnificent journey.

If the answer is a DEFINITE, CONGRUENT YES, then dream big and so it shall be!

Chapter 3

THE JOURNEY CONTINUED... INTENTION

David found himself at the foot of a cold rocky mountain and couldn't really remember how he had come to be there. He knew sometimes when he drank he would end up somewhere without having any memory of how he got there; could this be one of these times?

It didn't matter to him though, as he knew intuitively he was at the mountain his dad had spoken about.

He looked up but could not see the top of the mountain. All he saw was clouds and snow.

He couldn't see what his path was; he just knew his goal.

He looked for a means of transport up the mountain but couldn't find one; he looked for someone to guide him but there was no one. He searched his pockets and couldn't find any cash. He thought, 'How am I going to do this?'

With faith in himself, he knew what his intention was and he decided to step up to the challenge and begin climbing no matter what.

INTENTION

Defining an intention is one of the most powerful ways of completing any task, goal, job, mission, etc. It doesn't matter how small the task or how great the mission.

Setting an intention works within the Law of Attraction which I will discuss in the next chapter. It is the fuel that powers it!

When we set our focus on a particular goal and we add absolute determination to it, it becomes an intention of power that has the ingredients for ultimate success.

It is this definite purpose that gives us not only the power of our conscious mind but also our unconscious thoughts.

With an intention this powerful there's nothing that can stand in our way!

Chapter 4

THE JOURNEY CONTINUED… LAW OF ATTRACTION

At first, David found his mountain-climb difficult because he was not in a good physical condition. However, soon he realised that when he needed to make decisions it was like a path was being laid out before his eyes. It was like he had received some help along the way and learnt that he was more resilient than he thought.

He kept climbing and things were going just fine but as soon as he was getting comfortable his thoughts wondered off and he began thinking of how difficult the climb may really be. As he took a couple more worrying steps, the clouds got thicker and snow began falling even more, totally obscuring his vision. His thoughts had come true. He couldn't see where he was going and he stopped in his ascension up the mountain. These obstacles were too difficult to get through. He was stuck.

He took a cold deep breath and calmed his thoughts. He then told himself he would get through these obstacles soon if he followed his intuition. He climbed and climbed; it seemed impossible but he knew that his persistence would pay off.

As he continued to ascend the mountain his thoughts drifted and as he gazed into the falling snow he began thinking about his life and how he could make it better.

In the silence he began appreciating the so-called obstacles, admiring the peaceful white of the snow and the soft calmness of the clouds which gave him the opportunity to think more deeply. These obstacles weren't that bad after all.

He was not alone.

David noticed a little squirrel with an extra furry tail and a red robin that seemed to keep him company along his journey as well.

Every step he took, he had support from his little friends. He stopped, smiled at them, nodded and continued climbing and climbing.

After some time, the path seemed so long and things became challenging again. He became dehydrated and weak and was already halfway up the mountain but looked up and still couldn't see the top. He thought for a moment, this is impossible! He thought about turning back.

He looked over his shoulder, saw how far he had got and said, 'I'm not going back!'

He didn't go back.

He kept on moving forward.

He made up his mind and was now determined to get up the mountain no matter what. He needed to visit the wise old man to learn the secret of life.

As he took another step forward the unbelievable happened. As if the challenge wasn't tough enough, rain began pouring from the sky.

Feeling overwhelmed, the man closed his eyes and began to cry. He stood in the middle of a huge mountain, full of deep snow and thick clouds pouring with ice cold rain.

He closed his eyes and remembered something else his dad had said,

'Son, if you fall twice then get back up 3 times!'

David opened his eyes and looked around with absolute focus and determination and remembered his goal and purpose.

He remembered why he was climbing the mountain.

He then noticed a tree up ahead with branches like arms to shelter him. He ran to it and sheltered from the heavy rain drops.

Even though it was very cold, he felt such a warm loving presence from that tree. He felt a motherly love from it, as if it was an angel who was protecting him. He sat underneath it, knowing it would shelter him.

The tree had many cup-shaped leaves; they held pure water for him to drink. He smiled and drank the water appreciating the rain; the blessing in disguise.

When the rain had stopped he stood up, poised and determined and ready to climb again. He continued up the mountain, no longer dehydrated but now full of energy and purpose. He climbed until he could see the clouds below him. He was at the top!

It was so peaceful at the top of the mountain. There were snow covered trees outlining the almost circular surface area and a comfortable looking rock in the middle. He felt a sigh of relief and more importantly a sense of accomplishment.

LAW OF ATTRACTION

The Law of Attraction is one of the most powerful laws of the universe; it can be briefly explained as the ability to bring about whatever you think about and have feelings about.

The Law of Attraction is a universal law of perfection that works in synchronicity with your feeling centre – good feelings and bad!

Everything that exists has energy; it has a vibration. That is, everything you see is made up of energy that has a specific vibration, a frequency, density and an arrangement of subatomic matter. For example, a chair only looks the way it does because of its subatomic arrangement of particles.

We exist in a world where matter is formed from a field of pure potentiality. It is the thoughts and feelings that begin the manifestation process.

Every thought and feeling is electrical and magnetic in nature. This energy goes into the field of potentiality and with constant thought and feelings about this particular thing creation is sparked within this field or 'quantum soup'.

Thinking about something that you really want and feeling great about having it will start the creation process and the universe will align itself to bring this to you.

This also goes for someone that thinks about something they don't want and feels bad about it happening. The universe with its perfection will align itself to bring this to you.

Remember for the Law of Attraction to work for you, it is not just the act of wanting something in your life that makes it appear, it is feeling that you already have it, being thankful for it and most importantly, allowing it to come into your reality.

What does this mean?

When you want something that resonates with your feelings and you are already thankful for receiving it, the universe instantly aligns itself to bring this to you and with your enhanced awareness, you will see opportunities knocking at your door. This is when you need to allow it to manifest – open the door!

When we live from inspiration, our thoughts and feelings are incredibly powerful. There is balance, gratitude, purpose and positive vibrations. Any thought that exists with this resonating power behind it will undoubtedly be manifested into physical reality.

I have spoken with many people in seminars, groups and in private discussions where they talk about how they are not getting the things they want in life and are thus unhappy.

My first question is always, 'Well, what do you want?' The answer, most of the time, is,

'I just want to be happy!'

Of course, this is not a specific answer, and is without objectives. A better answer would be clear and defined, for example: 'I want to increase my spiritual awareness and connect to nature', or 'I want to find a job that allows me to travel'.

My next question would be, 'What are you doing to get more spiritual connections or new employment?' Usually the response is,

'Well, I don't have enough time to do that'.
Or,
'I don't know how to do that'.

If you truly want something, wouldn't you spend all of your time to make sure you get it?'

When we think of something we want out of desperation, the universe with its perfect Law of Attraction brings what we feel back to us; that is, when we are desperate for something we resonate in a vibration of lack, therefore we attract lack, but when we are inspired by something we resonate in a vibration of plenty, therefore we attract plenty.

In other words, we attract that which we focus upon, either consciously or unconsciously!

If we think about all the things that are going wrong in our lives or the things we just don't want, then this is what we attract to ourselves. It is a universal law.

If things appear to be going wrong, focus on what you want rather than on what you don't want. Focus on what you have rather than what you think you don't have. When you focus on that which you want, the universe will provide exactly that which you vibrate!

Here's an example: Let's say on a simplistic level there are 3 similar people who say they all want new jobs.

The first person repeats the fact that they want a new job as an affirmation 100 times a day.

The second sends their CV to a free job seeking website.

And the third leaves home with the goal of handing out 20 CVs in person that same day and has already planned how many he's going to deliver in the next week.

All 3 people want the same thing but all in different determination vibrations. They may all get a new job but the secret is, the person that leaves home that same day to hand out 20 resumes has a higher vibration of purpose than the rest and will be employed much quicker than the rest.

It is the definite purpose in this person that brings about the definite result! The vibration of this definite purpose will spark the creation process within the universal field of pure potentiality and manifest itself more quickly.

If someone is unemployed for a long period of time, it is probably not because they are not qualified enough to get the job that they desire, nor because they are unlucky or lazy, it is just because they have other priorities.

Their determination vibration for getting a job is not at the top of their list; therefore it will not be resonating in their reality any time soon.

You attract what you vibrate and resonate with and once you understand this fundamental law of the universe, you can create your own paradise!

Set your intention and spend time planning, meditating and acting upon it with complete and absolute conviction. This brings power to your intention. Also, think of it as a seed and give it the proper water and brilliant sunlight of inspired action it needs to grow!

Set this intention of power and feel great already knowing it's going to happen. Already know it's waiting for you and be thankful for receiving it and the universe will acknowledge you already have it! Therefore you will attract it!

Here is the Law of Attraction in short:

- Set an intention of power for what you want with true feeling
- The universe will align to your intention
- Be thankful it's already yours and you shall receive it... just allow it. (This may entail taking action when opportunity knocks).

Attract what you want and be grateful for already having received it! It shall be yours.

In fact, it already is!

SYNCHRONICITY

Have you ever said that you needed to get in contact with someone and all of a sudden that person contacts you? Have you ever thought about something then found that someone gives it to you the day after? Have you set an intention and noticed strange 'coincidences' during the day towards your intention?

These are all examples of synchronicity! They are all events that happen in flow with your intentions, i.e. your vibrations.

In my opinion, a coincidence does not exist! Calling something a coincidence takes the power out of the event and blocks gratitude.

Have you ever woken up at 5:55 in the morning without your alarm and noticed this same occurrence for a couple of days in a row? How about looking at your clock and it is 10:10? Synchronicity!

Have you ever dreamed of a number and seen this particular number pop up again and again throughout the day? There's another 7! Synchronicity!

When we take note of these synchronicities and appreciate them, we show an active gratitude towards our ultimate purpose, bringing even more great things to us.

These synchronicities tell us we are in the right direction to stepping onto our own unique path of fulfilment and it is by observing and appreciating these synchronicities that we emit the love frequency and hence bring more desired events our way!

When we see more and more occurrences that are clearly synchronistic events in line with our vision, we are on a path to manifesting what we want.

I remember once I needed to get an audio cassette converted to a digital format and had no idea how to do it or whom to go to. I needed it for the weekend and it was already Wednesday! I had already known about the Law of Attraction so I set my intention of power and began searching on the internet for people who provided this service. I found many but it was just too expensive and their time frames were too long. I even consider buying a tape deck to do the conversions myself. I then got a message from one of my clients asking if he could train later that night which was unusual and I said of course, and asked if he knew anyone that could do the conversion of the cassette to digital. What were the odds? Not only did he know someone, the equipment was in his office, his employee was an audio expert and he said I'll have it the next day! By Thursday night, I was already sipping tea, listening to the MP3 conversion.

Synchronicity also exists for the times when chaos seems to continue throughout your day or life.

Imagine that you get out of bed very late, walk straight into the door on your way out, then run to the train station only to realise you forgot your train ticket at home and to top it off it is raining and you don't have an umbrella.

You probably think to yourself: why is this always happening to me? Why do I keep attracting the wrong things into my life?

These are synchronicities as well! At times like this we must reflect and realise we are not on our path to fulfilment. These synchronistic chaotic events are the manifestations of suppressed emotions we are not dealing with and the universe has its very unique ways of expressing the imbalances to awaken us.

It is only after becoming aware of these signs, having a definite willingness to change and see the perfection behind the chaos, that you can neutralise and transcend these seemingly painful synchronistic occurrences into balance.

If you don't like what keeps happening in your life and it tends to 'always' happen, then bless it, thank it, love it and change your approach. When we suppress what we really want to do, we are going against our divine selves and life will remind us of this!

Open your eyes and heart and see the truth that is there. Synchronicity can be very revealing and powerful.

Look for the synchronicities in life and appreciate their messages!

Chapter 5

THE JOURNEY CONTINUED... DON'T CREATE LIMITING BELIEFS

David sat on the rock and wrote words in the snow with a stick he found. They read, 'I'm ready and willing to change.'

Having done that, he sat and waited. He had no idea what to do next but knew he was where he needed to be at that time.

Then, after a little while, an old man dressed in a cream-coloured thick hooded robe with golden leather sandals walked across the snow towards him and sat down next to him. David couldn't see his face because the shadow of the hood covered his entire face except for the tip of his nose. Surely this must be the person his father had told him to look for. David asked him,

'What is the secret to life? Where can I find love?'

The old man stood up slowly pointed to a far away mountain peak.

David looked at the old man's pointing finger and said, 'Am I supposed to find love there?' There was no answer so the man looked at the far mountain. He then said in confusion, 'I can't even see that mountain properly! It's snowing too much over there.'

There was no answer, but the man knew the old man was supposed to know the secret to life so he continued looking at the vaguely visible outline of the mountain hundreds of miles away.

After he had been staring for a long time, clouds came and covered the distant mountain completely. He turned to the old man and he was still looking in the direction of the far off mountain.

David then said, 'Ok, I can't find love there, so where can I find love?' The old man turned his back to David.

David became a bit concerned; he wondered if he had said something that had offended the old man. He stood there for a long time again and thought,

'Maybe I don't understand the message here.'

Again he asked the wise old man, 'Where can I find love?' The old man raised his finger and pointed but in that direction there was absolutely nothing but snow falling from the sky. David was now feeling impatient and confused. He assumed the old man was making fun of him. He believed he just didn't want to help him at all and walked away muttering, 'He's just a silly old man.'

DON'T CREATE LIMITING BELIEFS

Our experiences and perspectives determine our beliefs which we then use to make decisions about situations, people and things. Our filters strengthen these beliefs because they search for what we are unconsciously holding to be true. Unfortunately these 'beliefs' are one-sided views which have solidified themselves throughout time within our perceptions.

We go through life unknowingly filtering everything that we see, hear, feel, smell and taste. We are bombarded with so much information through our senses that we would go insane if we were to understand every aspect of just one second.

Take 7 seconds and try this: On this page, count how many times the word 'and' appears. Make sure you count each and every 'and'. You have only 7 seconds.

Start from the top now!

Now, after counting each 'and' tell me how many times did the word 'we' appear on that page. Ah, you thought I would have asked for the number of times the word 'and' appeared but didn't you see the entire page and also read each word? How about the word 'our' did you see how many times the word 'our' was used?

Interesting!

We only see what we are searching for and unconsciously delete the rest. With this, we have the tendency to make assumptions, create limiting beliefs and judge people and situations based on our limiting perceptions.

This is where we can misinterpret a situation and overlook the truth of what's taking place.

How many times have we judged someone because of their nationality although we haven't even met them yet? Or how about assuming our partner knows what we are thinking about when they really have no clue?

Not everyone has the same perspective as we do; nor do we have a full understanding of each story we hear. With our personal views we tend to fit people, situations and events into our personal paradigms for things to make sense. Everyone has a different view of the world!

The challenge here is, many of us hold our assumptions to be true and judge people based on limited information. This creates limiting beliefs.

We can ask a better question to avoid limited views that can create unnecessary tension between people, groups, nations, etc.

When someone acts a certain way remember they are just like us, trying to deal with their 'stuff', or maybe we just haven't understood the message yet!

Look for what the message is by asking questions. Maybe what we were thinking was right or maybe it was the exact opposite but let us not set ourselves up for potentially limited beliefs.

Do not judge a person by their colour, status, bank account, networks, etc. Judge a person by their heart.

Sometimes through speech, we spread toxic words about people or things to other people giving them an already twisted view on the real truth.

Can you remember a time a friend told you something horrible about someone you were about to meet and you didn't like that person before they even had a chance to say hello?

When we make assumptions about people and things, we tend to believe them. This is very dangerous. It is important for us to become conscious of it because it is these thoughts that create disharmony, false perceptions, imbalance and even wars.

Remember, assumptions are things we think are true with no evidence. We tend to create false worlds and unnecessary turmoil when we blind ourselves with these fallacies.

Do we believe that our bosses or the government or people that earn more money than us are better than us and we must feel lesser in their presence? Or can we rise above the labels, authorities and the system to appreciate that they are men and women just like us?

A person who earns millions a year is not necessarily happier than a man who lives in nature and earns nothing. It is only the belief that having money equals happiness which is a fallacy.

Your boss does not necessarily have a better life than you and celebrities aren't living perfect lives. These are all assumptions and they do not help us grow in our hearts or bring peace into our lives.

This is also true for our relationships. Do you assume you know what your friends and family are thinking with limited knowledge? Do you guess what they are thinking and believe it with certainty? Sometimes we are right but sometimes we are very wrong.

We can easily avoid creating these situations and having contaminated thoughts by appreciating everyone for just being who they are and having clear communication with whoever we encounter.

When we create limiting beliefs, we give room for unnecessary disappointment and also unfairness to the dynamic that can exist between people.

Sometimes we judge people unfairly only because we have insecurities about ourselves and look to discredit someone to make ourselves feel better. This is only a temporary feeling and a limited perspective. Become aware that the person is learning along their path as well and appreciate them for who they are.

We are all unconditional love souls looking for love and living in a world of duality.

FORGIVENESS

Forgiveness is a lesson we grow up with, taught to us by the ones we look up to. We learn to forgive our friends, families, strangers and anyone else that has done us wrong.

It takes a lot of inner strength and courage to forgive. Yet even though we have forgiven, have we really forgotten? Is it possible that whatever has happened sits deep within our memories and can surface later on?

Often, we have emotionally held on to the charge and missed the importance of what is really taking place.

It doesn't matter what anyone has done to us, whoever they are or whatever it may be.

When someone has done something that seems wrong or unfair, we can forgive them but there's something even more powerful with this event.

The key is to look for the lessons hidden within the event and see how it benefits us. In seeing the both sides of the equation there is nothing but gratitude and love.

It is more powerful to forgive, appreciate and thank the person who has hurt us for doing whatever they did rather than just forgiving them, which implies a one-sided wrong.

In this state of gratitude there is no emotional charge of wrong or right, there is a transcendence of judgment and a state of clarity and balance.

Everything that takes place has a meaning and purpose. They are all synchronistic events that happen in resonance to our vibrations. When we look for the truth, we will find it.

On a much deeper level, these are the lessons we have chosen!

Be grateful for the experience and learn from the lessons that are present at that moment.

Forgive, see both sides and be grateful and thankful for the experience.

Chapter 6

THE JOURNEY CONTINUED... DON'T TAKE ANYTHING PERSONALLY

David could still see nothing but snow. He looked back to the original far mountain peak where there was still nothing visible, then he looked and searched everywhere in every direction.

He started feeling that he was going crazy as he even searched on the ground and under his feet!

Agitated, he took a quick deep breath and walked back to the old man and said,

'When I look for love out there I don't see it!'

Again he walked away from the old man who still hadn't spoken a word.

He felt so ridiculous at that point and so all alone again, not even this old man cared about him and had turned his back on him like everyone else; he immediately sunk back into the thought that he just wasn't good enough.

DON'T TAKE ANYTHING PERSONALLY

Whenever we are criticised, ridiculed or made fun of we often, if not always, take it to heart or take it personally.

Just because someone turns their back on you, this doesn't mean you are taken for granted or unworthy of love, it simply means they are dealing with their own crises or there is something more to understand at that moment. If you look for the understanding you will find it when the time is right!

Sometimes we hear criticisms thrown directly at us and, understandably, these comments can hurt.

I'm sure you can remember a time when someone told us something like, 'You're an idiot!' or 'You're a waste of time!' or 'You can't sing to save your life!'

These things hurt our feelings and our filters look for circumstances to back these false beliefs up.

We can live with these painful burdens for the rest of our lives and our emotions become negatively charged, adding dark areas or spots on our souls making us become very heavy emotionally and limited in our self belief. We begin to lose our light.

When we begin listening to the opinions of others rather than living freely from our hearts we cause ourselves to be insecure, limited and fearful that we are not good enough.

We don't believe or follow what our hearts want us to do and end up walking on egg shells to please everyone else.

Remember, if someone says something hurtful to you, these are only one-sided views based on one person's perspective towards you out of approximately 6,700,000,000 people on this planet. I don't think that's too bad ☺

The great thing is that it's absolutely a matter of understanding what's going on and seeing it from another point of view.

If we know this, nothing can touch us! Remember, everyone has his or her own perspectives based on the experiences they had while growing up. They are all dealing with their stuff!

With these perspectives in place, they will unconsciously feel and act a certain way whenever a certain situation occurs.

This goes the other way too! If someone says you are a god or you are beautiful, do not take it personally. You already know you are everything! You cannot have a magnet with one side, it is the positive and negative that completes the magnet.

If someone says you're an idiot then smile and don't take it personally and if someone else says you're the hottest person they ever met then smile and don't take it personally either. Thank them from your heart and appreciate them.

If that person was intentionally seeking to hurt you and you don't take it personally, you give them an opportunity to reflect on what they were trying to do, and why.

You already know you are untouchable. You already know you are everything. Give them a chance to understand and grow!

If someone laughs at you, then laugh with them, it probably was funny (at least to them) so why not enjoy it and learn from it?

If someone turns their back on you, admire their lovely back and look for the message.

It doesn't matter who the person is, they can be a Prime Minister or a beggar on the street, a king of a country or a beach bum. Authority is manmade, love is not. Become your own authority!

One day, upon exiting a London tube station going to the gym I was stopped by a police officer checking people with bags. There was also another officer that came towards me as if to interrogate me and took my bag to check inside it. The questions began 'Why are you at this station?' 'Where are you going?' 'What are you doing in this country?' etc. I thought they were a bit harsh but I knew these officers were just doing what they thought was best and all I had in my bag was a Rubik's cube. Because I didn't take anything personally and instead admired them for their persistence, within 2 minutes, there were now 4 police officers around me asking me if I could be their personal trainer and if I could give tips on diet!

Whenever someone does something or says something hurtful to you, immediately think or say, 'Interesting!' or 'Impressive!' then look for what you can learn.

Be thankful, and give them the opportunity to think and learn as well!

Now continue being magnificent! Just don't take it personally ☺

LOVE THE SOUL, NOT THE LABEL

We all carry labels and put them onto other people and things. They work as a form of identification, and convey importance and significance.

The question is do we remember people for who they really are or for their label?

It is the essence of the person which you should admire and not the label. Some of us who have bosses say, my boss is the best! It's great to love your boss but understand that it's not because he is a 'boss' that makes him great, it's because he demonstrates that which a boss should be to you.

There are also some people who say they don't like their boss! Remember, the word boss is just a label; look at the person behind the label and love them for who they are.

How about our family? Do we love them because they are our family and we feel that we have to love them? Remember we do not have to do anything! Love your brother, mother, sister, father, teacher, etc, for who they are inside. Love and remember the soul!

These labels are only words of reference rather than the essence of inner beauty that can be found in each individual.

It doesn't matter if a man or woman has the label of officer, royalty, vendor, celebrity, bailiff, solider, baker, tax man, lawyer, etc, they all want to be loved just like us and they are all souls just like us. We all have labels but this does not define the essence of who we are inside.

Speak from your heart and see the magnificence of whoever you encounter.

Let us look at the person behind the label and let's respect them for their achievements. Speaking to a soul and not a label will yield us a response of truth, connection and willingness, instead of programmed responses of the illusion.

Chapter 7

THE JOURNEY CONTINUED… CONFUSION

David didn't give up so easily. He turned around and said in complete confusion, 'I can't find love outside there, how am I supposed to even know what to look for?' In frustration he continued, 'Where else am I supposed to look? If not out there then where else; in here…?'

There was only silence…

David stopped and looked at his hands; he was pointing to his heart.

He stopped and thought about what he just said, 'If not out there then where else – in here?'

'In my heart?'

Suddenly he felt a wave of pure light washing over him. He felt a sense of understanding and a connection to the truth. It was a breakthrough.

He turned to the old man and said, 'I need to find love inside before I can see it outside! I need to love and appreciate who I am!'

CONFUSION

If you're confused, get ready for something grand! It is in times of confusion that our mind looks for any possible way out. It looks both consciously and unconsciously for meanings, solutions and sense. It is in these times we can discover something that we've been looking for our entire lives!

Sometimes confusion can easily lead to frustration which is even more powerful. This means even more excitement!

If you're frustrated, celebrate!

There will be a breakthrough coming to you soon so be ready for it. The answer is right around the corner.

The important thing here is to ask better questions.

The better the question, the better the answer!

Instead of saying, 'Why is this happening to me?' say, 'How can I solve this?' or better yet, say, 'How can I solve this and enjoy it at the same time?'

Look for the inner truth, not the false surface. When we understand what is really unfolding we become centred, grateful and purposeful, leaving us inspired and present.

Chapter 8

THE JOURNEY CONTINUED… GRATITUDE

The wise old man closed his eyes and took a deep breath. He smiled.

Then he spoke in a very familiar voice, 'You now know the secret of life too, my son.'

The old man slowly turned around and removed his hood.

David saw his dad smiling at him, so peaceful, so calm.

'Sometimes my son, we see clouds and snow that seem to block us from getting where we want to go, it is then the squirrels and birds keep us company. They support us in these tough times. Even the clouds and snow have their purpose in these times as well.

Sometimes the rain washes away our hopes of getting any further along the path but it is then that the angels protect us and we can look for a blessing in disguise.

And, if you choose to continue climbing that mountain, the journey will be an adventure you will treasure forever. When you get to the top, you will feel a sense of accomplishment, a peace and fulfilment. Be grateful for your journey up the mountain and all its lessons along the way.'

GRATITUDE

This is the most important chapter in this book. True gratitude equals unconditional love and when we have true unconditional love we vibrate at the highest frequency: it is the key to all!

In quantum physics an event is just an event; it is our perspective of that particular event based on our experiences that makes us consider it to be good or bad. In other words, everything that happens is for a purpose and we can look for the synchronicities in everything and know that both positive and negative exist simultaneously in every single moment and event.

Duality is an integral part of life. Seeing both the positives and negatives in any situation transcends judgment and gives us gratitude for each experience, which allows us to have unconditional love.

At this point, I'd like to share a couple of stories from my life which will give you an idea of how we can change our perspectives and transcend the bi-polarity and be grateful for anything and everything.

As an 11-year-old, I was told I didn't have much longer to live because of a stomach condition which limited my ability to eat and to digest food. I was not like a normal child; I was always at the doctor's office, and I was very shy, quiet, ill and weak. I was too weak to even open the fridge door properly.

At 14, I was 55 kilograms and already over 6 feet tall. I was slow, and my peers laughed at me for the way I looked.

You probably feel sorry for me and pity me? For good reason... but if I could go back in time and change something, I would change absolutely nothing! Why?

Because of this seemingly 'bad' experience, I decided to learn everything I could about the human body and how to alter its shape, performance, strength, balance and posture. It is because of this 'blessing in disguise' that I was able to go on to teach and influence thousands of people to live their dreams in the areas of health, fitness and nutrition. I've seen total changes in body shapes, health conditions and postural alignments and I have been told time and time again that I have added joy, confidence, understanding and wellbeing to their lives.

I still train and educate people in fitness and nutrition because it gives me such pleasure and fulfilment, which not only brings health and wellbeing to the people I work with but also joy to me.

Every person is so very special and I get such energy learning from these people about their experiences and their lessons in life. This gift of sharing knowledge and seeing lives change before my eyes is priceless!

This is living from the heart.

Now, let's go back to my childhood stomach condition. I was often in pain and at home missing my education. As a result, I had to repeat an entire year of school and because I was so academically behind, I was told that I was not very smart.

I remember saying things in my head like, 'Why am I so stupid?' 'Everyone thinks I'm slow and stupid and you know what, they're right, I am!' I told myself the worst things possible.

That experience taught me something though – that I learn better not in a classroom but on my own or with a friend. I decided to relearn English and practice my language skills while hiding in my room.

I became so obsessed by learning I taught myself to remember at least one or more phrases not only in English but in over 40 languages, even Morse code and Braille.

Today, I have German phrase books and a German dictionary, Italian phrase books, Spanish dictionaries and Spanish phrase books and Spanish story books, a Russian dictionary, a Portuguese phrase book, Egyptian hieroglyphics, French phrase books and a French dictionary – all in just one of my drawers!

With this so called 'adversity' I'm now able to converse and connect with many people from different cultures and have a deeper understanding and communication with them. I never thought I would be a person that would be able to speak with people generally and be able to shine my light.

I went from being an extreme introvert to becoming qualified as a stage presenter and Master NLP practitioner!

I couldn't read well either so I decided to step it up a notch there too. Before I read a couple pages per hour and now, not only did I learn how to read but I can speed read 250 page books in less than an hour and a half and teach what was in that book immediately after. I even read upside down, sideways and in reflections just for the fun of it.

My eyes opened to a world of quantum physics, spirituality, psychology, neurolinguistics, astrology, esoteric wisdoms, sacred geometry and much more. I felt such inspiration in learning about life and beyond life.

However, it was the studying of universal laws that really got me to understand the gifts that we possess. It was that adversity that gave me this joy!

Now tell me whether this really a bad experience or blessing in disguise? I like to think about it with some light humour and say, thank God I was 'slow' ☺

If not for this experience this book would also have been just a thought or probably not even that. It is the understanding of both sides, positive and negative, that leaves us in a state of balanced gratitude which in turn transcends any emotional charges on our souls. We see the love that always exists.

Having gratitude opens the heart and emits unconditional love to the universe and back. It leaves us vibrating at the highest frequency attracting only like vibrations back to us!

Always remember the key to love, that is, the universal understanding of the word love, is having gratitude for both positive and negative sides, therefore transcending all judgment and living from the heart.

Chapter 9

THE JOURNEY CONTINUED… WE ARE NEVER MISSING ANYTHING

David hugged his dad with tears of joy and fulfilment in his eyes. He had just learnt that he needed to love himself before he could expect anyone to love him, to follow his heart and he would get support along the way, that obstacles are only temporarily in his way but would somehow keep him on the right path and also that if he asked the right questions, he would find the right answers.

Still hugging his dad he said, 'Please don't leave me again, Dad, please don't,' and his dad responded, 'I never did and I never will. Always remember you are never missing anything, it just may appear in a different form and when you look for it, you will find it. Love yourself, love everyone and everything without judgment and see the magnificence that you are. It will be then that you bring the same back to you.

Always remember, love is all there is.'

WE ARE NEVER MISSING ANYTHING

When we think we are missing something it is only an illusion.

We have everything!

We are never missing anything; it is only in a different form that we haven't appreciated yet! When we do appreciate something it appears, and when we think we are missing something it evades us because of the universal flow of energy.

Remember if we believe the idea we don't have money, love, friends, health, etc then we shall receive exactly what we believe – which is not having.

Let's look at an example of money. I remember a time when I had very little money and the number of clients I had was very low. I realised I was doing too many things in my life and lost focus on keeping a steady client base. I decided to apply this understanding that we are never missing anything.

I counted the number of clients I had, took my appointments book and got a clear picture that I could do so much more. I knew I had skills to offer and appreciated this and I also knew what times I was willing to work. For every hour I didn't have a client within a possible time slot I wrote, 'New Client'. I then calculated how much I will earn with the new schedule and felt really great about it. The fact that I appreciated my ability and created the intention of power with gratitude, the next week I already had 4 new clients rather than the previous couple months with no new clients. This is the power anyone can create just by taking an active role in realising nothing is missing. Of course I was also thankful for the previous months for having extra time to do my other projects!

Take some time and look for where you already have what you are looking for. Make sure you see exactly where you have this value even if it's in a fragmented form and then be grateful you already have it. Take an active role in realising nothing is missing. As a result, you will no longer resonate in a vibration of lack.

It is this gratitude that switches the dynamic from not having something to creating the vibration of already having it. This creates a difference in the flow of universal energy.

If you are an artist and feel that you do not have enough money, look at your paintings and ask yourself, does my work have value? I am certain it does! Appreciate that you already have value. If you look for where the value is, you will find it. From the moment you realise you have this value, you will be inspired and ideas will come to you. This is where you act upon your inspiration, that is, open the door! You may find a gallery you can put your painting for sale in with free rent space.

When there is appreciation and value for oneself, you will attract circumstances and events which equal this vibration. Value yourself, you're worth it!

When we value ourselves, the universe vibrates with this energy and values you. So if you need money, look for where you already have it and the moment you realise that you have it in some form, the universe vibrates this 'like energy' back to you.

Remember that opportunities will knock at your door once you are inspired by what you are doing and appreciate that you are never missing anything. When you realise you've got it, then it is yours. Remember to open the door when the universe knocks!

If you're looking for a relationship, then look for the traits you want in a person then see which people around you have these traits.

Remember, it can be in many forms! If you are looking for someone that has a good job, is attractive and independent then look at all the people in your life. You will find that probably your best friend has a good job, your boss is attractive, and your flat mate is independent. It doesn't matter if they are male or female, what does matter is that you appreciate that it is already in your life and look what happens next ☺

Sometimes things take time to see and understand but when we actively look for the synchronicities, the gifts within them become more apparent.

We have everything; we just need to look for it and appreciate it and it shall appear in a non-fragmented form.

We are complete!

Chapter 10

THE JOURNEY CONTINUED… VALUES

David was now grateful for everything in his life. He felt a pure love for his wife, his friends, his job and his family. He was fulfilled, inspired and at peace.

He felt like he was truly a magnificent person.

He decided at this point to dedicate his life to teaching what he had learnt on his journey. He now knew what was most important to him and his purpose was clear. He knew he had been through the things in his life for a greater cause, the bigger picture, his true purpose in life.

No longer was he looking for love on the outside, he already had it on the inside! He always did, he just never appreciated it.

He now understood everything has a reason, synchronicity, perfection, balance: the universal expression of unconditional love.

VALUES

Values are the things that are most important to us. They are the things that drive us and determine our direction in life.

When we live life by our true values, we live an inspired life attracting the right people, events and things at the right time. This is the universal law.

Some people say that it's such hard work to do what they really want to do!

My answer is, when you love what you do and do what you love, nothing is hard work.

When I do 5 hours of researching and writing, I never consider it to be difficult and that's because I'm doing what I love doing.

When we live from our highest values, life becomes an epic adventure. Wouldn't it be exciting to wake up every morning with a question like, let's see, how I can save the world today? I do! ☺

We all have values and priorities in life. Ask yourself this question:

What are the most important things to me?

You may respond by saying, 'Definitely being healthy, my family, my career, etc.'

Now let me surprise you by suggesting that this may not be the case!

Time and time again I've come across people who are living to make their parents proud, their boss happy, their partner satisfied, their friends to like them, or just to survive, but seldom do I come across someone that lives from the inner voice, the voice of truth, the voice of love and inspiration.

To give you an example, my highest values are learning, teaching, connection to all, and health and fitness. I know you may be thinking, how did I come up with this and how can you find out what your values are? I'm going to give you an easy way of finding this out for yourself.

For each question below, write at least 5 answers!

Have you ever realised that there are some things that make you feel really good? Really driven? Really inspired!?

1. **My first question is what inspires you or what makes you feel great?**
   What is that one thing or few things that can get you to open your eyes at 6:00 in the morning without an alarm clock with total excitement? What can you be doing for hours and hours and forget to eat but still feel full

of energy? For me, writing this book was a true inspiration because my purpose in this life is to share knowledge and teach people about their magnificence and guide them on an inspired path of truth. I wrote the words of this book at every possible hour you can imagine, when I was at the gym training, even while walking outside, while travelling and even while eating. I would open my eyes each morning with new words to add. You see, when something inspires you, your mind automatically thinks about it both consciously and unconsciously! (Write down at least 5 things that inspire you or make you feel great!)

2. **The second question is what do you constantly think about?**
   What is always running through your thoughts? Is it the person that you love? Your work? A creative expression, such as art or music? Food? Be honest with yourself, no one's looking! ☺ I am constantly thinking about philosophical ideas, about dimensions outside that of physical reality, mysteries of the universe and universal laws in particular.

Mostly, if not all of the time, I'm looking for something to learn or comprehend on a greater, more in-depth level. Remember, nothing is wrong or right; if your thoughts are similar to mine then that's great and if they are absolutely different then that's excellent. The world would be a boring place if we all were the same! (Write down at least 5 things that you constantly think about).

3. **The third question is what would you spend money on even if you didn't have any?**
   Have you every realised at some point in time you had very little money or were even in debt and you would still somehow find the money to buy that one thing that you really wanted and didn't really need? For example, you 'had' to buy a shoe because it was on sale! Justified right? ☺ I know I would always find the money to buy healthy quality food and crystals, and also to pay for my gym membership! Take a moment and think about 5 things for which you would actually go as far as borrowing money from a friend to get. Remember to be honest with yourself. (Write down at least 5 things that you would

spend your money on even if you didn't have any!)

4. **The fourth question is what do you fill your surroundings with?**
Look at your bedroom or favourite room, look at your computer desktop, look at the things you collect. What is your space filled with? My room is filled with crystals, spiritual books and learning materials, research sites on my internet browser bookmarks and my diary. I wake in the morning and meditate. I bless the day and everyone I can remember at the time. I then walk to my desk where I pass some spiritual books on the floor which I just like having there, then I turn on my computer to research some more quantum fields of study, universal laws or listen to channelled messages from star systems. What do you have around you? Do you have pictures of your family or loved ones? Art work hanging on your walls? Books on romance, quantum physics, business, etc? Food wrappers? Schedules and business materials? Look carefully and notice even when you clean your room you still leave

certain things on your desk or in plain sight. (Write down at least 5 things that you surround yourself with).

5. **The fifth question is what do people know you for?**
If someone was talking to another person about you, how would they describe you; what words would they choose to use? Would it be, 'Yeah, that guy that does yoga and is passionate about nutrition' or 'Remember that really quiet guy that used to work here and always ate potato chips for lunch?' or 'Remember that girl, the one that fed squirrels in the park even if it was raining?' Think about this for a moment. How do people describe you? What do people know you for? People tend to meet me and say something like, 'You have such a calming and peaceful aura and you look so focused, do you practice some sort of martial arts or something?' They often associate me with calm, balance, focus and dedicated physical practice. The people who know me would describe me as determined, peaceful, fit and knowledgeable. (Write down 5 things that

people know you for and be honest with yourself!)

6. **The sixth question is what do you spend your free time doing?**
   It doesn't matter how busy we are, we always have some free time. You may say this is not true and you don't have time for anything apart from work, or your children, but think about this. Is it that you don't have time for anything or that you don't want to spend time on the things that don't interest you? Ah! Remember, if there is something that you don't have time for, then most likely it is not at the top of your value list. Would I spend time watching television? 'No' not even 5 minutes! Would I spend time in meditation? 'Oh yes!' Time ceases to exist at that point. What would you do no matter how busy you may be? Play Sudoku? Check stocks? Listen to the radio? Watch television? Eat? Read? Look for UFOs? (Write down 5 things you spend your free time doing).

These value questions will be quite revealing for some. I believe knowing our values is the first and most important step in discovering what our purpose is and also how to really live life with balance, peace and joy.

Values can change with time and you can change your priorities if necessary.

In the 6 questions I got 38 answers

- Learning came up: 10 times
- Teaching came up: 9 times
- Connection to all came up: 14 times
- Health and fitness came up: 5 times.

Therefore my first value is connection to all, my second is learning, my third is teaching, and my fourth is health and fitness. Remember, these are just a few of my values but they are the primary ones.

These are the true values that will determine your destiny!

When you have your values written down in front of you, look at them and ask yourself, 'Am I living by these values?'

If your answer is yes then you are on the path of your life's purpose and your destiny is your chosen one.

If you are not living by these values then you most likely have inner conflict and are living to please others rather than yourself.

If you don't like what you see but it is correct then let this act as an eye opener and know that it's time to start listening to your inner voice. Become quiet and honestly ask yourself, 'What do I really want?' Then gradually begin to shift towards your true life's purpose and your innermost desires.

When you live by and respect your values, you are honouring and loving yourself, therefore you vibrate at the highest frequency and draw that which resonates with this frequency back to you. Also if you are not living by these values, you will vibrate at a lower frequency, therefore attracting that which resonates with that frequency back to you.

This is the perfect law of the universe, the Law of Attraction.

Here is a quick way of finding out if you are living according to your values. Ask yourself this question:

If someone wrote you a cheque for £10,000,000 what would you do as a career or as a hobby?

If the answer is exactly what you're doing now, then you are living according to your values and the path to fulfilment!

If your answer is everything else except what you are doing now, then there is an imbalance and inner conflict: you are probably working to survive, and living in the illusion rather than working to express your soul's purpose.

You see, it's not money that's important, it's your inspiration. Money fills needs!

Inspiration fills the heart!

If someone gave me £10,000,000 right now, I'd put it aside and continue writing this book!

I would prefer to live in a shack doing what I love doing with the person I love by my side rather than living in a mansion alone with a false identity.

It is your life and you can decide which path you are going to take. It is never too late!

The question some of you may be asking now is can I change my values? The answer is yes!

I remember at a certain point in my life, I needed to travel to a specific place every day and really didn't want to.

I asked myself, what can I do to enjoy this? It was a forty minute journey to the place and another forty minutes back; I decided to look at what could I possibly do in this time.

This is when I looked at one of my highest values and decided to find books on quantum physics or spiritual development which I could speed read during this time.

I began getting excited at just the thought of gaining more knowledge in this time and of course with the Law of Attraction being so perfect, I was given books to read from friends without even asking. I was now enjoying the journey and didn't want it to end.

In order to change your values, associate the value you want higher in your list with the value that's already at the top.

I'll give you another example: If you don't like your day time job as a bank teller and your highest value is singing, then set an intention of meeting a customer in the music industry! Have an internet video of you singing on a website and when that person comes along, with synchronicity, and opens up a conversation about music, give them your website and contact details while staying balanced and grateful.

Now you'll be going to work every day looking forward to every person who steps into your line!

Remember the power of intention and set out clearly what you want in your mind. The Law of Attraction will do the rest, just allow it to flow!

Now you have your values and with this your purpose will become clearer and clearer if it is not apparent already.

Every soul has a higher purpose. It is the experiences of duality that shine light on our path, and in appreciating both aspects of positive and negative gives us the vision to see what our true magnificence and purpose was and still is.

We all deserve love no matter what we have done and there should be no regret for what we have not done!

See what your values are and learn and love from every experience you have had, good and bad. See how it has guided you here to the point you are at now and be grateful for the lessons and excitement of where you have now chosen to go!

You have decided every step to reach where you are today! Therefore,

It is time to decide where your next step will be!

Chapter 11

THE JOURNEY TO A NEW BEGINNING

David heard his name being called. He looked up and around and could only see the white of the snow. He was still hugging someone but he couldn't see who it was and the mountain where they stood was now becoming very vague.

He heard his name being called and he opened his eyes wider. The snow had stopped and he could see more clearly what was around him.

All of a sudden he took a deep breath and his vision came back fully.

There stood his mother, his best friend Luke, a girl with wavy red hair he didn't know, a doctor and the person that was hugging him – his wife Hanna. He realised he was looking at the white walls of a hospital room.

The doctor, who was very old and wise, came up to him and said in a calm voice, 'You had a serious heart attack. Your wife came home to collect her things and saw you with a picture of your dad in your hands; you were unconscious. Luckily she got you to the hospital in time. You slipped into a deep coma for a couple of hours but you climbed your way back to the top and you're now stable! What a journey you must have had.'

David smiled and hugged Hanna with pure love. Luke came up to him and said, 'Hey, good to have you back. I knew you'd find the way!' His mum stood behind everyone with a warm loving presence like an angel. The doctor then said, 'OK, let's give this man and wife some time alone.'

Before Luke left, he introduced the red-headed girl as his new girlfriend, Robin. She said, 'Nice to meet you; I'm glad we could be here to keep you company and give you support.' She then said, 'Look at what your friend got!' She held up Luke's arm and pulled up his shirt sleeve and showed him a tattoo of a little squirrel with an extra furry tail and then they all laughed. The doctor laughed as well and said, 'OK, OK, let's go now'.

David hugged his wife tightly to him and said, 'Please don't leave me again, my love, please don't.' and Hanna then responded, 'I never did and I never will'.

We are never missing anything!

Love is all there is!

PART 2

With this new understanding about ourselves, excitement takes us to the question, what's next now?

Now we are willing to change and feel grateful for our lives, knowing that we are everything and everything is love, let us now live the adventure according to our true life's purpose.

This second part is a combination of more empowering guidelines and lessons to discovering the secrets of enjoying a more inspiring and fulfilling life.

Chapter 12

7 AREAS OF LIFE

Life can be categorised into 7 main areas: Spiritual, Mental, Financial, Social, Family, Relationship and Physical.

The balancing of these areas helps us to enjoy our personal freedom and experience love, prosperity and fulfilment to our highest levels.

Spiritual

Our spiritual area is the part of ourselves that searches for the answers to life, wants to connect to the higher source, has faith and belief in God, believes in the existence of a divine intelligence and guides us to meditate. When we have a developed spiritual area, we tend to be calm and at peace, always accepting circumstances around us and within us knowing we are everything and everything is us.

Spirituality has nothing to do with religion; it is the understanding of one's spirit, the infiniteness of our being and the essence of self beyond the physical.

When we are spiritual, we tend to have or do some or more of the following:

We tend to meditate or pray, have visions, be at one with nature, ask life philosophical questions, look for the balance in everything and look for our purpose seeking a means by which to express it, sometimes through music, art, dancing or teaching.

Connect to the divine, become enlightened and spread your light.

Mental

Our mental area deals with our enthusiasm for personal development, intellectual research, logical thinking and heightened learning. This area has to do with psychological balancing and it is also the area that deals with emotions and the way in which we cope with situations.

When we are mentally inclined we tend to be driven by learning, are good at memorising, enjoy researching information, think logically, question things systematically, and come up with better ways to solve issues, being analytical, observant and strategic.

Learn as much as you can and use your intellect with heart.

Financial

Our financial area relates to our job, career, passive income (money we earn on our spare time) or whatever we do for money.

When we are financially driven we tend to be accurate with our personal accounting, do more to get more money, have a proper budget system, invest, and pay bills on time.

Being financially driven doesn't necessarily mean you have money, it just means you are driven by the idea of making money.

You can have a lot of money and not be financially driven as well. It all depends on what your goals and circumstances are.

In a later chapter, I will discuss finance in more detail.

Be grateful for money; but remember that it should be a by-product of what you enjoy!

Social

This area has to do with our interactions with people, how we communicate, and going out and other social activities.

Do you avoid communicating? Do you prefer staying at home, socialising in quiet places and one-on-one interactions?

Or do you enjoy speaking with new people, partying, saying whatever you're thinking at that moment, going out, and are always on the phone and chatting on the internet or posting an hour by hour commentary of what's going on in your life?

Everyone communicates differently. Interact with love and without judgment.

Family

This area deals with our closeness and connection to our family.

Do you speak to your family every day? Once a week? Once a month? Only at Christmas?

There are people who will do anything for their families and will visit them quite frequently, and there are some who haven't seen or heard from them for years.

It is great to have a close connection to your family but never a dependency. They are there to support you and guide you when the time is appropriate and also vice versa and realise that you never have to live for them, please them or make them proud.

When you do what most inspires you and you live from your heart, you already please them, make them proud and inspire them as well.

If you don't have a good connection with your family because of past circumstances, remember them in your heart for who they really are and neutralise the experiences that may have caused you pain with gratitude.

We all are expressing our ways of being from our experiences and perspectives. Each person is unique and at a different point of their journey. When we are grateful for them and we neutralise these bi polarities, we reconnect with them on another level transcending judgement and realigning us back to the truth and love that was, is and will always be present.

Always remember where you come from!

Relationship

This area deals with relationships between couples and relationships between friends.

With respect to partner relationships, some of us are quite content with one love while some of us are unfulfilled in this area and go from partner to partner.

There are some people that are with a partner and want to be with many and also some who are afraid to be with anyone. There are so many circumstances that lead to disharmony when this area is not fulfilled and it is so important to find peace and harmony here.

The act of sharing our lives with another is a blessing and is a means of expressing our divine nature, sexuality and creative energies.

Remember it is important to share your life with someone, but never give it to them and never depend on them. Both individuals in a relationship are of equal importance and it is appreciating each other for who they are that provides the balance that brings love.

The same goes with relationships with friends; do you constantly make new friends or do you have a core group?

Some of us have so many internet and phone contacts but yet feel so alone. Looking for acquaintance with many may cause you to lose the essence of real friendship. It is great to have friends but make sure they are real friends that appreciate the real you.

Whether you share your time with your partner or friends, value yourself and others will value you!

Health

The area of health also includes physique and beauty and has been taken for granted by many. We tend to wait until it's too late before we take our health into consideration.

Some people completely overlook the importance of nutrition. It is possible to have a good looking body and be unhealthy!

This also goes the other way. Some of us eat very well but do not exercise at all. It is possible to have great health and be out of shape.

Nutrition is a very important aspect of health. Proper intake of vitamins, minerals, fats, proteins and fibres will enhance and regulate your system to function at its best. When we function at our best, we produce the best and we live at our best.

Nutrition helps our internal systems, brain and body functionality, hygiene and connection with ourselves and others.

Exercise is also a very important aspect of health. When we exercise we get in shape, increase our stamina, align our posture, increase endurance, enhance vitality and improve movement. We also gain more connection to our spiritual being, sexuality and become more attractive.

Exercise can be done anywhere and can take less than 10 minutes a day. Find out what works for you!

Some of us love the gym, some love going for a jog, some expand their physicality and spirituality through yoga and martial arts, and some climb mountains. Choose what you really enjoy; who knows, maybe it will be all of the above!

Beauty is also in the physical area. That is, buying fashionable clothes, perfumes or aftershaves, make-up, shoes, spa treatments, facials, pedicures, manicures, physical enhancements, etc. It's always great to look your best and feel your best.

Eat for excellence, exercise for performance, shop for fun; you're already beautiful!

Here's some fun stuff to do: Write a list of exactly what you want to improvement on in each of these 7 areas to fulfil your aspirations!

For example:

- Spiritual – Meditate more, be in nature for peace and connection
- Mental – Take a course on internet marketing, learn a new language
- Financial – Save money, buy quality investments
- Social – Meet new people, network with likeminded people
- Family – Keep in contact more, visit them more regularly
- Relationship – Find that special someone, date more
- Health – Begin jogging, eat fresh organic foods

Make sure your list is inspiring to you!

Now, choose at least 4 of those areas and take a small but definite step of inspired action in each.

Let's say you choose spiritual, mental, social and health!
I will give examples of the very simple steps that can make all the difference.

- Spiritual – Choose 1 day a week to spend an hour in a park relaxing.
- Mental – Set aside 10 minutes per night to learn 3 new words in a new language.
- Social – Join an online group of likeminded people and meet up with them once a week.
- Health – Jog on the spot once a day for 10 minutes.

Every little step counts and makes a huge difference after a period of time. Just think of a one month period: In one month you would've spent 240 minutes in a park relaxing, learnt 90 new words in another language, probably met over 25 new people and also jogged 300 minutes! Imagine what can be done in 3 months!

Have fun with this and take those small steps to big dreams!

Chapter 13

BE GENUINE

With our minds so influenced by what is wrong or right in the eyes of others, it is easy for us to get caught up in what we think is right rather than what we feel is right. We tend to do things and act a certain way to be accepted by others.

Do you tell yourself that you really want to do something but are really doing it because someone else expects you to or wants you to?

Are you honest with living your life or do you live it to please others?

Do you answer questions from your heart or with responses people want to hear?

The ironic thing is, the more we do things according to our real feelings the more we are understood and the more we are respected, and not the other way around!

When we follow the crowd we become lost in it, but when we value our opinions and speak them we become leaders.

In an office, many people are fearful of the 'boss'; in their presence, they often stand straighter, pretend they are doing something important, try to look engrossed in work, and sometimes even their voice changes when speaking to them.

Isn't this all false? Fake? Fear?

Let's say 2 years passes by and you ask your boss for an increase in salary. The typical response would be, 'No, the company does not have the budget for that right now' or just simply, 'No!'

I'm sure we all know someone who has had this experience.

Now, imagine in that same company, there's a new person who doesn't stand any differently when the boss approaches him; he does his work the best he can; he respects his boss and speaks with him as a real person. Now, isn't this genuine?

Let's say 6 months passes by, do you think the new person would ask for an increase in salary and get it?

No! He wouldn't even have to ask!

When we value, love and respect both ourselves and others, the universe vibrates this frequency back to us. When we are false, selfish and fearful, the universe vibrates this frequency back onto us.

Being genuine gives you freedom!

It is not only showing honesty towards someone else but being honest with yourself.

Haven't we all been asked how things are and we automatically respond, things are great, work is good and life's wonderful, while we really feel like crap on the inside and probably want to go home and cry every night and say why me?

Let's be honest, let's be genuine, and let's replace the automatic responses with genuine words spoken from the heart.

When we are genuine we respect ourselves and others. When we are honest there is nothing to hide. When we speak the truth, we are valued.

Be genuine and you will be valued and respected.

Chapter 14

BE YOU

Sometimes it can be confusing when in certain situations people don't acknowledge us or pay attention to what we are saying. They tend to take us for granted.

I remember once I was speaking with someone and they said, 'whenever I start talking about personal development and consciousness to my friends they don't take me seriously, sometimes they even laugh at me and ask me if I'm OK. Why?'

What is happening in a situation such as this is very important and straightforward. The question is, 'What type of energy are you giving off?

If someone dedicated their life to a specific topic, for example personal evolution, and they studied it and pondered over it all the time, it would be clear in that person's aura, vibration and personality that they knew what they were talking about, lived by it, and believed their thoughts 100 percent.

If someone met me in a meeting or group and they didn't know me, they would probably say, 'I guess you don't drink alcohol so would you like something else… water perhaps?' They would know, without having to ask, that I don't drink.

Remember, your true vibration is felt through non-physical means and if you practice and believe what you are preaching then your audience will be fully engaged; the only reason they wouldn't be interested is if they were just not ready to receive the knowledge and you should respect them for this. It may not be something that's at the top of their values list. It is just not their time to learn, or it is not your time to teach.

Be grateful for the lesson and know that you will emit a unique vibration of who you are to everyone that sees or hears you.

Sometimes there are people we admire and look up to and sometimes there are people we scorn and look down upon.

Remember, it doesn't matter if you're a king or a beggar! We all are souls learning at our own pace and are travelling on our own paths looking for truth.

Love and appreciate the king and the beggar the same, for they give a dynamic balance to the equilibrium.

Learn from the people you admire and teach those that truly would like to learn from you. The goal is never to be just like someone else, the goal is to be who you were meant to be. You!

If you meet me and say, I want to be just like you, then you miss the point. If you meet me and say, I would like to learn from you, then you have understood! Do not worship me nor walk behind me, because I am no greater than you. Nor am I less than you.

If you want to learn from me then walk with me as my friend.

Remember to do what inspires you and not what temporarily amazes you, or what someone else says you have to.

Follow your heart and not the ego or opinions of others and you will find the master who's ready to teach you.

Be inspired! Be centred! Be you!

Chapter 15

IMPRESS YOURSELF

When you leave home do you do everything possible to look good for whoever may see you?

Do you sometimes hide from people when you don't look your best and even do drastic things to avoid people seeing you?

Do you automatically feel bad when someone looks at you a specific way and tells you that you look different today?'

In all of these examples, we are living by the judgments of others rather than the acceptance, love and gratitude of ourselves, for who we are.

If you leave home saying, 'Yeah, I look hot!' even if your hair looks like it had been in an explosion, you will have such a light carefree approach and love for yourself that people will magnetically be attracted to you. Who knows, maybe your hair may open a conversation with someone you really like!

It is not about comparing yourself to others but about being the best you can be.

Do your best and be the best you can be!

When we do what we love and love what we do, there's no one person's opinion that can affect us, be it good or bad. We will already be resonating at the love frequency because it is our inner voice that we follow – the voice of our hearts.

Learn as much as you can, sing as loud as you want, conquer mountains, and live your life as an epic adventure.

Impress yourself!

Chapter 16

VALUE IS NOT WHAT YOU HAVE

I remember when one day I woke up feeling frustrated with the way things were going in my life. My relationship wasn't going well, my income was low, my training partner had disappeared and my business was nonexistent.

I was so distressed that I thought I was going crazy.

I remembered going to sleep that night thinking, 'What is it that I'm not getting here? What is the message?' I went to sleep that night and woke up the next morning with a strange answer. I looked around my room and said, 'I'm going to give away everything I don't need, use or want.'

I had a quick breakfast and took a deep breath and began. I went through my drawers, cupboards, bathroom, everything I possibly had, even my pockets and suitcases.

I couldn't believe how many things were just piling up which had no use to me.

That day I ended up with 2 suitcases full of stuff to give away! I packed everything neatly to give to charity and also put up for sale some equipment I didn't need any more. I was amazed how many things I had collected along the way.

I had so much baggage!

I didn't realise how much I was carrying around; actually, I didn't even realise that it was all there!

When I had got rid of my baggage, I felt a lot lighter and at peace. I felt more focused and full of purpose, and ready to live my dreams again!

How many of us have baggage in our homes? How many have it in our lives and hearts?

How many of us drag this heavy baggage wherever we go, even though we don't need it and it is cluttering up the place?

Let's get it sorted!

Be grateful for what it has brought into your life and let it go. We don't need things that clutter our 'space'.

That day, I gave away 85 percent of my things and felt so much better. I then realised I was frustrated because I had lost focus on what my purpose was – to help and teach people. Giving away my stuff was helping others and woke me up to this lesson.

I was now wealthy with the infinite and not cluttered by my 'stuff'!

I now valued myself and knew that I had everything within me.

That same night, all the things that seemed to be missing came back. My relationship was suddenly brilliant again, my business was back on track, my training partner reappeared and my finances improved!

I understood the true lesson, which was the value was not in what I had but in who I was. I was so caught up in all the clutter and the baggage that I lost focus on what was most important.

I realised great people like Mother Teresa and Mahatma Gandhi could have made a million if they wanted in a day but they wouldn't even want it. They could give away everything and have it all back in a night. It was the value they had as a person that allowed them to acquire their wealth. Their value was not in what they had but in who they were.

We all have this value, even if we are not famous; we just need to see it and appreciate it.

When we live from inspiration and the expression of love, we become like a magnet and draw in whatever we need, whenever we need it.

It is not the buying and selling of properties that makes you wealthy, it is not the cars in your driveway that give you value, it is not your position at work that identifies you, it is living impeccably by your purpose with gratitude that makes you wealthy by God; when you're wealthy by God, you function at the level of masters.

- Let go of what you don't need!
- Neutralise the emotions which weigh you down like excess baggage!
- Make space for the new!
- Express who you are!

The value is not in what you have, but in who you are!

Chapter 17

CREATING SOMETHING FROM NOTHING

How many times have you let a great idea fade away because you thought that you didn't have enough money to pursue it, because you didn't feel confident about what you were doing, or because you thought that you didn't have enough time to dedicate to it?

How about if that same great idea was done by someone else who now has a great business doing exactly what you wanted to do? How would you feel?

This happens so often in the world today because of fear and disbelief in ourselves. We fear that our idea is not good enough, believe that it will be laughed at, fear that we need money we don't have, believe that it'll take too much time to do what we want... and the list goes on!

The wonderful thing is that it's possible to get a project completed with little or no money, enough time and to create opportunities for others to live their dreams while fulfilling yours.

Interesting?

We all have abilities, skills and talents whether we choose to believe so or not. We all have ideas that to some can seem laughable, or hard to imagine. Yet no idea is ridiculous, no question is silly!

Remember that when we vibrate an energy of insignificance, desperation and lack, so we shall receive; however when we take our talents, skills and abilities into account and we value ourselves then we are playing a much bigger game. When we act from our inspiration and gratitude, we emit these vibrations and attract the same. Let's begin!

Firstly, think of one thing, one project, or one task that you would love to accomplish because it's something that inspires you, and write it down. Give it a cool code name to add an element of fun to it, such as Project Top Secret!

This objective and intention must be in line with your purpose!

It doesn't matter how big or small your goal; what matters is how you value yourself in comparison to the project.

If you believe you can handle it and you are ready for it then you are!

I will guide you through each step and show you how much fun it can be to achieve something that previously seemed overwhelming.

Remember our reality is created by us; let's make it extraordinary!

I will use an example of a project to give you tips and more understanding.

My objective was to get a workout video completed.

Code Name – The Ultimate Body DVD.

Purpose – To teach proper exercise and to inspire people to get fit.

Next, write down all the things, people and resources you need to get the project completed! It doesn't matter about the order, so write down every possible thing that comes to you in this moment on that page.

When I did this I wrote with both hands and used different colour pens. Remember this is something you're inspired by, therefore the list should flow until your pen is empty or you page is filled ☺ Here was my list to give you an idea:

- Things – Camera, lights, script, structure
- People – Cameraman, editor, friend, team
- Resources – Gym space, equipment

Next, write down the skills, talents and abilities you have, plus anything else you can think of, that might help you to achieve this project. Here was my skills, talents and abilities list:

- Knowledge of proper exercises
- Ability to communicate
- Ability to visualise project

Now it's time for action! You've already done your objective in line with your purpose, your 'to get' list and your abilities, etc.

You have already begun to attract this goal!

It's very easy to realise when the attraction process starts; it's the moment you begin to feel excited about doing what you're inspired by!

Put the list in order of 'most important' to 'not necessary yet'.

Now, get a friend on board!

This is where things get really fun; if you have someone in mind, go for it, if not then wherever you go, talk to people. In conversation, people generally ask what you do. Just mention that you're working on a project and the things you're looking for to complete it and *voila*! Sooner rather than later, if you're truly inspired by your objective, they are going to be inspired too and will know someone that can help or they themselves may like to be a part of it.

It is also possible to post an advertisement with an exchange of your skills for someone else's free of charge. You'll be amazed at how many people will be interested in your project! This is the law at work.

Trust it! Flow with it!

I mentioned my project to a close friend of mine before I even had my list completed. I told him what I wanted to accomplish and within twenty minutes we were working on a workout DVD! He knew I was inspired and purposeful therefore he was inspired and driven by the vision! He was the perfect person for me and the project.

Note, my only precaution here is to make sure the person or group of people you choose to work with are inspired by your vision rather than merely hyped-up by it. This is very important; make sure they have a balanced perspective on the project rather than a lop-sided, elated approach to what they can gain.

Next, delegate tasks to your new 'business' partner or everyone in the group you've conjured up, including yourself, and have frequent meetings.

Delegation has nothing to do with commanding someone to do a task, but rather at looking at the skills that person or each person in the group has and giving tasks to them which they already love doing!

Do you see how great this is so far? Not only are you working on your dream, you now have a bunch of inspired people loving what they are doing working towards your dream as well! Here were my friend's delegated tasks:

- Implement deadlines
- Take care of formalities
- Keep account of formalities
- Make calls

My delegated tasks:

- Write out all 220 exercises to be performed
- Draw concepts for the layout
- Perform exercises

Meetings took place every day in person, on the internet and over the phone at specific times and we fine-tuned the project whenever necessary. It was good fun plus we continued having separate lives.

Obstacles may seem to appear!

It is important to flow like water in your approach, always moving and creating new paths along the way. No obstacle is a dead end; it's only an opening to another direction!

Next, it's time to get things in place! When it is time to put the puzzle pieces together, things may not go exactly as plan; this is where most people stop but others find a new route to success.

Now, depending on your project you may need more people, resources, money, equipment, etc. It may seem like a tough stage but it's actually quite fascinating. This means you're getting closer.

My friend and I now had the blueprints for the workout DVD and a clear vision in mind. We began interviewing film crews and explained to them the whole concept of the vision.

After a couple of weeks we had interviewed 5 film crews and the costs were just ridiculous. We thought how is it possible to get this money to shoot the DVD?

We had an obstacle and were unsure of what to do next. A few weeks later, we backed down and thought, 'Well, it was a good idea but maybe it's not the right time'.

At that moment we said, 'Hold on!' We remembered our original feelings about the project, and our objectives and purpose. Obstacles? No, we just needed to see the message and remember the purpose.

We saw how easy it was to slip into a downward spiral and quit. But we didn't.

All fired up, we reset our intentions of power and were ready for the universe to perform its wonders.

Within a few days the universe came knocking at our door. I spoke about my project to a client of mine and he happened to be a brilliant cameraman with professional equipment! He also had access to lights and was an editor. Now that's what I call synchronicity!

He was inspired to shoot and edit the DVD in exchange for my skills and knowledge as a trainer!

My friend also attracted many people willing to help us who wanted nothing more than to be a part of it!

We got lots of support along the way, assistance from friends, and help from people we didn't even know. We were very grateful and stayed balanced.

Within a couple of weeks the DVD was completed for the price of what we would spend on a typical restaurant dinner instead of the price of a new car.

Whatever your project is always remember the following guidelines:

- Have a clear objective in line with your purpose
- Write a list and prioritise
- Expand your team with a friend or group of people inspired towards helping you achieve your vision
- Delegate tasks
- Meet at structured intervals in person, online, or on the phone
- Flow like water around any obstacles

- Exchange services if necessary
- Look out for synchronicities and be grateful when they arrive
- Live your dream.

Whatever you would like to create, there's always a way, there's always someone that wants to be part of your journey, and there's always more than enough resources!

If you would like to produce a song then record yourself singing something with anything you have to hand, even your mobile phone video camera, and post it on a website that does exchanges of skills. There are many new sound producers needing to gain experience who won't charge you for working together.

If you would like to model, send photographs of yourself to upcoming photographers looking for experience and you'll get a good portfolio to show to agencies.

If you would like to start a dating site, then search for a web designer, lawyer and sponsor who are all single! ☺

It doesn't matter how big your project, you can create something from nothing!

Chapter 18

PASSIVE INCOME

Finance is one of the areas that often come up when people are in need of guidance. Let's take a look at passive income.

Sometimes it seems difficult to leave our existing jobs to do what we love doing with the feeling of no backup, no guarantee, no security or stability. We have many responsibilities and bills to pay on time.

Here's the secret!

When you know for certain what your inspiration is and you know it's in line with your purpose then it is time to put things into action for it to manifest.

Let's create some examples to work with and I will show you the magic of being able to pay off bills and still create a fortune!

Let's say you're a qualified accountant working for an accountancy firm and your true dream is to be a nature photographer.

Most of us don't leave our existing jobs to fulfil our passions because it seems too risky.

Fortunately, there's no risk at all!

Get your camera out, grab your laptop, pick up a notepad and let's go!

When you know you are working on what inspires you, your energy is limitless! No television is necessary, no newspaper interests you and you can't wait for every new day to begin!

With your camera in front of you, you probably want to start shooting your living room just because you love photography, but before shooting let's get a structure in place.

Ok, so you want to be a nature photographer!

Great!

- Use the internet to look for concepts, angles and styles of images you want to replicate and save these images to a new folder on your desktop and call the folder something that resonates with you, e.g. The Dream Lives.
- Now, look for images of landscapes, animals and nature near you or within your location. Write these down.

- With the images of these areas, choose and prioritise which you like most and number them.
- Set a date and time on each location and think of a style and write it next to the date and time, e.g. Saturday 6:00 pm, magic hour, 20 mm polarizer filter style. These are the missions you're aiming to complete.
- Take the new folder with the images (The Dream Lives), transfer them to your phone or print them small on a page or two; probably 30 images on each side.
- Find a site that will allow you to create a photographer's profile that you can sell your photography on and they will most likely take a percentage, which means that you take the rest.
- Clean your camera lens and charge your battery!
- SHOOT!
- When you get to the location, complete the exact image you envisioned before shooting anything else! You can always look on your phone or printed sheets to remember the style.

- Come home, don't stay on top the mountain ☺ edit your photos and choose one or more that portrays your skills and vision and upload it to your new photographer's profile.
- Draw a line through the first location on your note pad and write Mission Accomplished.

Now you have a system in place, you have the locations to shoot and images to sell, and you're still paying your bills with your normal job! And that is just the beginning!

Here's where it gets interesting. As you take more and more pictures, the possibilities of people buying your photographs will also increase.

There could now be a taking-over point where your inspiration earns you more than your income!

See it, appreciate it and flow with it. You will now be able to live fully from what inspires you, and within a short time you can work on what you love and leave behind what you had to do to survive.

You may well be able to hold your own exhibitions, charge more for your photos, possibly teach your new trade, and leave a legacy of who you were really meant to be!

Give it a shot!

Think about what you're inspired by and start making a passive income from it.

Some of us like doing things for free but always remember that when you value your service, others value it as well. If you give a service for free, it is sometimes taken for granted and under-appreciated. By putting a value on your services, you place a value on yourself and this will earn you respect!

This is an incredibly exciting adventure that leads to the path of fulfilment. People around you will love to join you!

With things going according to plan, be grateful, appreciate the synchronicities and stay in balance.

Passive income is the key to financial riches.

Here are some very important questions to ask yourself to know if you are on the path to financial fulfilment.

- Do you work because you love to?
- Because you want to?
- Because you have to?

With respect to passive income do you work long hours because of a hobby that inspires you, or because you need to do it to survive?

If you love your job then brilliant, if you love your career then perfect, and if your passive income comes from inspiration then you've mastered this area.

I believe this will be an eye opener for many as finance is the major issue in the world today. It is one of the main reasons why people are unfulfilled in life.

Why work so hard just to survive rather than doing what you love and money is the by-product?

Tap in to the river of wealth, it flows from the heart!

Chapter 19

WHAT CAN I DO OR WHO CAN I HELP TODAY?

This is one of my favourite questions. It brings such service, joy and sharing to life and in return has so many more hidden gifts. The average person thinks, 'What can I get from this person if I do this or what can I get for free?' This is a very one-sided equation and leaves the other side unfulfilled.

The good thing is, after reading up to this point, we aren't average anymore! ☺

When you wake in the morning with an intention such as, 'What can I do to help someone today?' then you automatically vibrate a vibration of plenty and not only do you find someone you can bring some joy to, you also bring plenty back onto you with the perfect Law of Attraction.

Giving from your heart or helping has nothing to do with the giving of money, as some may think. You can give a genuine smile, a sincere compliment, good advice or even offer some of your lunch; it can be anything! Once you genuinely give without expecting anything in return, you get back genuinely without the expectation of having to receive anything back. It is the flow of energy; it is the Law of the Attraction. In doing this we spread love and light and give people the opportunity to learn and do the same.

I remember when I began doing this – it was so much fun and still is. I would go to the supermarket and ask the cashier how their day had been and they would look at me, smile and answer straight from the heart.

That 5 to 10 second interchange may have changed that person's day, including mine. They believe that someone cared enough to ask them about their day and as a result, it vibrated in their essence and opened their hearts, which may have filtered through to the person next in line.

It is the spreading of light, the emanation of love. When we give from the heart, we clear negative charges and spiral pure vibrations upwards. What can you do?

- Compliment someone on their clothes!
- Spend some time listening to others!
- Say 'thank you so much'!

Today, let's see who we can spread our love and light to ☺

Chapter 20

LANGUAGE FOR LIFE

Life's a gift!

We have the tendency to automatically answer certain questions without much thought or say things without much consideration!

This can be dangerous because unknowingly, this has a great psychological effect on us.

We grew up hearing what others say and this influences us to respond as we think we should, saying what others want to hear or what sounds right! Seldom do we actually say what we are really thinking because we are afraid we may say something incorrect or offend someone.

When we go through life using words, language and metaphors that are disempowering, we unconsciously lower our frequency and unknowingly become disempowered.

This is also true when we use empowering words! When we speak in a positive tone we unconsciously raise our frequency and become empowered beings of purpose.

Let's take a look at some of the most common phrases people use which can led to negative states:

- I have to
- I can't
- I should
- I have no choice
- I think I can
- I'd like to go but
- I'll try to do my best

I've discovered through my experiences and research how much freedom we give away just by the words we use.

For a moment, think about your language and if what you say empowers you or not. For example, would you say:

- I have to go or I need to go?
- I can't come or I won't be coming?
- I should lose weight or I will lose weight?
- I have no choice or it's best that?
- I think I can' or I believe I can?
- I'd like to go but or I don't feel like going?
- I'll try to do my best or I'll do my best?

Can you hear the difference?

Let's set ourselves up for a win each time with our language. Let's leave the disempowered language of fear behind, it doesn't serve us. We're too good for that!

How many times have we heard someone say:

- Life's so hard!
- Life just isn't fair!

If you engrain this language in your daily speech then so it shall be.

Have you ever seen a pattern in the people that say these things? They are most likely to be unfulfilled in their lives.

How about someone who genuinely says:

- Life's a gift!
- Life's so amazing!

Here too, there will be a pattern to the people that answer this way, they are much more carefree and enjoy living.

Whenever we have tough times, we can turn the dynamic around just by the perspective and language we use.

If someone shouts at us, it's just because they have stuff to deal with. Bless them and ask a better question, such as 'I wonder what happened to him? Maybe he needs someone to talk to about something!' See them for who they really are, a soul on a journey looking for truth just like us.

Remember, don't take anything personally!

If something happens that doesn't seem fair or in your favour then say, 'Interesting!' Make it fun!

A couple of years ago, I had a birthday celebration and someone said, 'Wow, you're one year older now!' I smiled and said, 'Interesting, I believe I'm one year wiser as well!'

Look for the fun and balance in everything!

If you're frustrated with something say, 'Bring it on!' you already know it's time to celebrate! ☺

Chapter 21

MEDITATION

From a very early age, I've been fascinated by the metaphysical realms and spirituality; that is the concepts and knowledge beyond normal physics, especially consciousness, dimensions and altered states; for example, Lucid Dreaming (the ability to be conscious within a dream).

Some of these practices have led me to deeper states of existence and experiencing dimensions in and outside that of physical reality.

My initial meditations were what some would consider haphazard or simply unfocused; sitting in silence having no idea what to do, just remaining still while hoping for something miraculous to happen.

In my twenties, I began appreciating the importance of real silence and began to understand that noise did not only come from outside sources but was also internal and in my opinion, more internal than external.

Internal noise can be defined as thoughts that pop into one's head without one consciously being aware that one is thinking about them until they are blatantly obvious. They may be events, situations, issues, ideas, and perceptions which can cause a lot of internal conflict within oneself.

In this chapter I will describe and explain the most powerful meditations I have done which have helped me to focus, have clarity and a deeper level of purpose.

Just to give you an idea of the techniques I've tried, here's a list of some:

Meditations with frequencies (sounds and tones); music; chanting; visual aids; synchronized body movements; in nature; contorted body positions; crystals; healing stones; visualisations; breathing; self-hypnosis; physical tension to relaxation; and even under-water meditation.

After having a full understanding of what silence really was, I became able to appreciate the real power and purpose of meditation.

Here are the guidelines I believe are necessary for a successful meditation:

- Before any meditation have a clear intention! This in itself will already set the universal forces into motion and begin the powers of attraction to your purpose.

- Choose your perfect time! There are morning people and there are night owls. I am a night person and sense a high degree of tranquillity and connectivity very late at night or more specifically during the very early hours of the morning, that is, my perfect time is usually between 2:00 and 4:00 in the morning. I also do another power meditation most mornings as I open my eyes and breathe in the metaphorical new beginning with my clear intention. It's always a good idea to have a set length of time that you set aside to meditate. Start small and work your way up to half hour periods.
- Choose an area which feels good to meditate in! Whether it is in your room or office it will work once it feels right for you. When you find this place, do not have your back facing any doors. I've noticed it adds some degree of disturbance in my essence. Be somewhere you can just be!
- Rid your place of any distractions! That is, switch your mobile off, unplug the phone line and turn off all electronic devices in the room. I do notice a higher sense of

connection when I do this. I find it very helpful and so do many other people.

Position: you can either be seated or lying down. I do both, at different times. The only important thing to note here is to keep your body in a posture that is comfortable. If you are sitting, keep your feet flat on the ground with a straight back not leaning on anything, with your hands on your thighs and your head slightly tilted up; if you are lying down, keep your body straight but natural. Most importantly, be comfortable. Also, if you are familiar with crystals and healing stones feel free to use them.

Now you are ready to go into a deep state of meditation.

I will walk you through 3 of my preferred meditations.

A meditation for silence, clarity and focus

This meditation is very simple to understand, but takes some practice to get through it successfully. It may take a few attempts, but you will get it!

This meditation is to quiet the noise in the mind and bring clarity, focus and awareness back to the present, the NOW. In mastering this meditation, you'll find it much easier to get jobs done easily and quickly, be focused on what's important and be purposeful in your approach to things.

With your eyes closed count every breath you take.

With every inhalation count one then let it go then inhale and count two then let it go again. If you can make it to 10 on the first couple of attempts great! Your target should be 100!

When you have accomplished this, you have mastered this meditation and can also successfully create and manifest things and events much more rapidly than others. It is the stilling of the mind and body that allows one to be more determined and successful.

A meditation for expanded awareness

This meditation will heighten your senses and dramatically increase your awareness. I strongly suggest turning your phone off as any noise will be radically amplified.

With all the steps in place for meditation, close your eyes and start listening to your own breathing. After about a minute start realising the sound of and feeling the beat of your own heart. At this point you may feel your body actually moving as a result of your heartbeat. This is good!

Next, listen to every little noise in the room and at the same time, observe the silence which may now become audible. You may hear a hissing frequency sound!

Now it's time to go beyond! Hear all the noises that are on the outside of the room, i.e. in your flat or house, then hear the noises outside – the dog that's barking, the car that just drove past, the plane that is flying above, etc.

And now the fun begins. In this expanded state and in your mind's eye, project yourself and walk out of the room you are in. Leave where you live and see every detail as you float past it.

Choose a destination you are familiar with and go there. At the speed of walking, follow your normal route, seeing everything. The trees, the dog that was barking, the colour of the cars that pass... and take a look up at the sky to observe the next plane.

Smell the coffee if you pass a cafe, or feel the rain drops if it is raining... and continue to wherever you want to be! You can imagine anything.

Also, if you are travelling on public transport, e.g. the train or bus (not if you're driving them), leave the seat and propel yourself upwards to the point where you can see the train from above. You may know the route you're travelling, therefore recreate the tracks or roads. Add in anything that is on the outside like cars, trees, a motorcycle or people, and just observe.

This meditation can be done for as long as you like and you can go as far as you like. It takes some imagination, hence the reason for using a route you are familiar with, or you can create your own adventure! Enjoy!

A meditation for confidence and readiness

This meditation is great for confidence. If you have an interview coming up, a performance or a meeting, this meditation will benefit you a great deal.

With all the previous steps in place quiet the mind with a couple of deep breaths, and then close your eyes.

Let's say there's an interview coming up!

See the interview step by step. See the clothes you're wearing, see the interviewer and hear the sounds in the room; hear the questions being asked and hear your answers to them. Stay balanced and calm through using your breath at all times. Even see your hands, the documents on the desk and feel the temperature in the room.

Next, see the interview again but this time through the eyes of the interviewer! See how you look, your posture, clothes, body language, eye contact and the position of your hands. Hear what you answer and see how you look when you answer the questions. See and impose confidence onto you.

Now, see the interview from a third person view that is just above you and a little behind. See how the room is laid out and extend your energy field of comfort into this room. Again see your clothes, posture, and the interviewer's questions, your answers and the reactions to them.

The key here is to envision exactly how you want it to be from all different perspectives, giving you the edge when the time comes.

You've already been there, you've already done it!

Meditation has been an integral part of my everyday life and I do at least 1 hour a day. Some days I do over 4 hours and the results are profound.

Choose an intention, meditate on it and see the magic that takes place.

Chapter 22

HEALING

Healing is a major aspect of life which is too often taken for granted.

In this chapter, I will shine some light on this area to give an understanding of how powerful we are. I could probably write another book on this subject because there's so much to be expressed.

We can heal ourselves; we can heal others; and hence we can heal the world!

When we listen to our hearts and follow our inspirations we experience physical reality as heaven on earth. This is the experience we are meant to have!

When we do what others want us to do and when we let the opinions of others affect and influence us, we suppress our emotions, our essence and our being, closing the pathways to expressing our true selves.

When we get to the point where the suppression is too much, our bodies take that emotional frequency and manifests it physically into our physical bodies. This is further amplified if our health is also taken for granted which is usually the case. How it manifests is unique to each person; that is why so many different conditions exist.

When we are not living according to our inspirations and we allow the toxic words of others to affect us, it is then the body makes an attempt to wake us up to the truth. It is then illness becomes rampant, conditions start appearing and in worst case scenarios, life threatening conditions will develop.

The conditions I'm referring to are the conditions that begin from stress-related events.

These conditions may seem like something negative but it is actually positive and the perfect expression of love. The body is perfect and when emotions are suppressed, unhealthy foods are eaten, lifestyles are threatening, etc, our body acts as an alarm to tell us that we are doing something that is not in our best interest. The body is waking us up to the truth so we can see that we are not living from a state of inspiration.

If you have experienced a condition that seemed to have appeared overnight or to have showed up for no apparent reason then this is the time to stop and seriously think about this aspect of your life.

Here are some keys to curing most stress, emotional or psychosomatic condition.

- Set aside some uninterruptable time to quiet the mind and have a clear intention to begin dissolving the condition. Remember you must be willing to change! (This will normally take 5 minutes of meditation).
- Acknowledge the condition, trace it back and trust that you remembered when it began! (5 minutes).
- Be grateful for it and understand its purpose and benefits! I know this may be a difficult thing to see at first but this is the cure. When you can actually see the positive things it has brought to your life, it may neutralise the emotional charge it needed to create the condition in the first place. Ask what it has positively brought you from the moment it began up until now! Write down the benefits, at least 10! (10 minutes).
- Appreciate the experience and the benefits of this condition! For this step, look at the benefits you've written down and for each one, replay in your mind and see the times

where you experienced these benefits and really be there and enjoy them! (10 minutes).

- Now instead of pain and suffering for this condition you will now have a love and gratitude for it! This is very important! This condition, this signal, this self-balancing act of unconditional love will then unlock itself from all of its symptoms as it regresses back to its purest state of balance and love. Gratitude is the key here! (Spend 10 minutes to reflect here).

When you can be truly grateful for the experience and love it, your condition has no need to wake you up to seeing the truth.

You see, it is the suppression of one's unconditional love that causes the body to do something radical in order for us to see that we are going against our deepest feelings for our true selves.

I know a girl that had a very hurtful relationship and refused to speak about it with anyone. She chose not to voice or deal with her experience and therefore kept it buried deep within her heart in a negative state of polarity. Her experience was so traumatic that she never wanted to be in another relationship believing that the same thing would happen to her again. The emotions were so intense and so suppressed that within a short period of time she developed a thyroid disorder.

As negative charges grow within, the filtering system in the brain searches for the proof to solidify the false belief, making it become more and more suppressed and as a result, may manifest itself into a physical form to wake us up to the truth. It can be anything because of how unique the emotional frequency is to everyone.

If someone told me I was insane, I would appreciate the time it actually took for them to express that, while someone else would probably take this personally.

If someone told me I couldn't sing, I would still do it if it was in my highest values. I would love the fact that after singing a song, someone may love how I sang, end up singing my song the entire day or laugh their heads off. Any way I look at it, I provide entertainment for them, which is my purpose for singing in the first place, plus I am doing what I love doing!

Never suppress your creativity, your spark or your source of love. Know that when you do what you love, you vibrate this essence in your being and this allows no reason for dis-ease or stress to occur. You will now be expressing your true light!

The same goes for conditions resulting out of poor nutrition and harmful lifestyles. Take a look at what the condition has brought you, be grateful for their presence and change your patterns. If we neutralise the condition within our hearts and continue to suppress it or we continue to have a poor lifestyle then our bodies will continue to send us perfect signals to wake us up to the truth.

Not every condition or dis-ease is a result of suppressed emotions or poor nutrition but our bodies send us incredible signals that we can learn from and heal ourselves with from becoming responsible and active towards this purpose.

Respect your body, take responsibility, listen to it, and see the perfection in its signals.

Know that your body always and perfectly functions out of love and it will do what is necessary to show you the truth. The condition, after being grateful for it, will release and dissolve itself!

We have the power to heal ourselves and regenerate our bodies.

When we understand the immortality and power we possess, we can live in absolute harmony with all.

It takes a grateful heart, balanced mind, conscious spirit and the willingness to understand the true purpose for these supposed afflictions.

With this transcendence of the physical self, knowing that the purpose is much larger than physicality, we can unlock these adversities to transform into miracles. We will exist in the infinity of divinity.

We all carry the healing frequency of love and light,
it just needs to be realised.

SUMMARY

The universe is infinite and so are we. We are all souls on a self chosen journey of duality, seeking the love that we already possess.

As humans we forget the infiniteness of our spirits and are likely to get caught up in physical reality as it appears to be. This is the illusion!

This is perfect, this is what was intended. We all feel there is something greater, something we were meant to do... and at some point in time we search for this.

Our purpose nudges us along the path that we ought to follow but often our intellect or logic gets in the way.

Think from the mind and live from the heart.

As we go along this journey to find our magnificence we awaken to who we really are if we ask the right questions and listen to our hearts.

We awaken to the truth that we are infinite beings and remember the unlimited self. We awaken to the truth that there is nothing but love in the universe. This is the equilibrium.

We all have profound power which can lead us to god-like states and abilities beyond the constructs of human thought.

When we listen to our hearts and function from inspiration, universal energies align and flow with us. We are here to create, to experience and to enjoy!

We are all unconditional love beings having a physical reality experience and once we realise this we experience joy, bliss, harmony and an unlimited capacity to create, love and share.

This is the original purpose of humanity, to live in unity!

Once you are grateful for both the positives and negatives in life, you will be balanced and complete, able to transcend human suffering and experience divine love while living through inspiration.

When we are awakened to the truth, the media has no effect on us, the governments cannot control us, opinions won't touch us and authorities will not scare us. We will be in a state of gratitude for the equilibrium that exists. Fear will not exist.

The more people on the earth that have this same vision and understanding, the more the earth will heal and humanity will become more united while all else dissolves because there is no need for us to wake up as a collective body.

Balance means gratitude for both sides of what has occurred.

The human is meant to create harmony, as is the entire universe. A balanced person means no inner conflicts, a balanced country means no crime, a balanced world means no wars, balanced worlds means a completed galaxy, and balanced galaxies means a completed universe.

- Love is the answer to all!
- Love is the key to infinity!
- Love Is All There Is!

Now go and write your life story of magnificence, choose the experiences you want to have and the life you want to live, and remember to leave your immortal stamp for others to follow in your enlightened footsteps.

THE END

THE NEW BEGINNING...